THIS

D1368411

THIS IS THE EMERGENCY PRESENT

VINCENT PAGÉ

TORONTO | COACH HOUSE BOOKS

first edition

 Canada Council Conseil des Arts
for the Arts du Canada
 ONTARIO ARTS COUNCIL
CONSEIL DES ARTS DE L'ONTARIO
an Ontario government agency
un organisme du gouvernement de l'Ontario
Canadä

Published with the generous assistance of the Canada Council for the
Arts and the Ontario Arts Council. Coach House Books also acknowl-
edges the support of the Government of Canada through the Canada
Book Fund and the Government of Ontario through the Ontario Book
Publishing Tax Credit.

LIBRARY AND ARCHIVES CANADA CATALOGUING IN PUBLICATION

Title: This is the emergency present / Vincent Pagé.
Names: Pagé, Vincent, 1989- author.
Description: Poems.
Identifiers: Canadiana (print) 20190141409 | Canadiana (ebook)
20190141425 | ISBN 9781552453995 (softcover) | ISBN 9781770566217
(PDF) | ISBN 9781770566200 (EPUB)
Classification: LCC PS8631.A345 T55 2019 | DDC C811/.6—dc23

This Is the Emergency Present is available as an ebook: ISBN 978 1 77056
620 0 (EPUB); ISBN 978 1 77056 621 7 (PDF)

Purchase of the print version of this book entitles you to a free digital
copy. To claim your ebook of this title, please email sales@chbooks.com
with proof of purchase. (Coach House Books reserves the right to
terminate the free digital download offer at any time.

~~VIENTE~~

XX

Tonight for example
the verse revolves
in blue

Shivers kind of

To have lost my voice
and loved her
without stars

I have her in my arms
but do not have her

This nearer distance

I write
this the last
endless verse

XIX

Has the wheat braided you into the brook
of its body?

It bears the wave in the field
the slender
the lithe

The wheat
bears the drunkenness of the plump bee

Everything of butterfly

It bears the mouth arms eyes curls
of girl

the dark if
of poppy

XVIII

Days
like phosphorus
unfurl in the water

I wrestle myself
among the cold things

The sound
is a port / is a sound
like *I love you.*

Look at me with your eyes!
I've forgotten how to grow

Night hides you
in the wire of its arrival

The coldest thing
among the cold things

XVII

Tangling in images
thinking how far from the city

your forest is
violent with the fog of fire

Curl toward the oh! up there!

Sparkle-shadow-sea-spray
bury my face

XVI

Wine dyes my regard
mourning colour

I go shouting at a cloud
so the dreams
are wide and sour

Nocturnal huntress
believe you me

how I love
them sweet feet

XV

I heard you in stillness
Silence emerges from silence

Because of what's absent
HEAR MY TALK

I am happy
Am I happy
I am happy
Am I happy

I sealed your bright mouth
now lamenting sound doesn't reach me

Are you happy
You are happy
Are you happy
You are happy

I need for you to be

come filled with voice

XIV

A cluster of lightshadow
and you existed

crammed against the power of men

Every day your suffer
does to me
what wind does
to loose boats

slaughtering my last-night name

You smell of rainwater
because I love you

Please don't shut your window shut

XIII

I have lived across the atlas
of your sadness

driven by a something
ravenous and still

You harbour water
and I'd love a few drops

Nets don't hold my thirst

But grapes
A delirious season

XII

You and your absence
undermine my sleeping

Your cupped
and taciturn will

In you
the freedom of birds
arriving like a wave

Here I gather the I

At times I've said
I am sad

At times I've said
You're an old road
The illusion of horizon

XI

Let's see how many eyes
and runaways

scatter the sleepy fury

Lily!
I CAN SAY NOTHING

Almost mountains
you were made of mountains
muddy girl

crazy stars / crazy dew / crazy wind / crazy wheel

You go without stopping
on the side of the road

cross longing
tasselled cloudless root

Ah! Smash everything you were

Carry off who you have so far
this side of her

sliced so there are sides you can touch

Muddy girl!
You're what I've come for

twentylovepoemsandasongofdespair.1bodyofawomanbod
yofawoman,whitehills,whitethighs,youlooklikeaworld,lyin
ginsurrender.myroughpeasant'sbodydigsinyouandmakest
hesonleapfromthedepthoftheearth.iwasalonelikeatunnel.t
hebirdsfledfromme,andnightswampedmewithitscrushing
weapon,likeanarrowinmybow,astoneinmysling.butthehou
rofvengeancefalls,andiloveyou.bodyofskin,ofmoss,ofeager
andfirmmilk.ohthegobletsofthebreast!ohtheeyesofabsence!
ohtherosesofthepubis!ohyourvoice,slowandsad.bodyofmy
woman,iwillpersistinyourgrace.mythirst,myboundlessdesi
re,myshiftingroad!darkriver-beds,wheretheeternalthirstfl
owsandwearinessfollows,andtheinfiniteache.IIthelightwra
psyouthelightwrapsyouinitsmortalflame.abstractedpalemo
urner,standingthatwayagainsttheoldpropellersofthetwiligh
tthatrevolvesaroundyou.speechless,myfriend,aloneinthelo
nelinessofthishourofthedeadandfilledwiththelivesoffire,pu
reheiroftheruinedday.aboughoffruitfallsfromthesunonyou
rdarkgarment.thegreatrootsofnightgrowsuddenlyfromyou
rsoul,andthethingsthathideinyoucomeoutagainsothatablue
andpallidpeople,yournewlyborn,takesnourishment.ohmag
nifecentandfecundandmagneticslaveofthecirclethatmovesi
nturnthroughblackandgold:rise,leadandpossessacreationso
richinlifethatitsflowersperish,anditisfullofsadness.IIIahvast
nessofpinesahvastnessofpines,murmurofwavesbreaking,sl
owplayoflights,solitarybell,twilightfallinginyoureyes,toydol
l,earth-shell,inwhomtheearthsings!inyouriverssingand
mysoulfleesinthemasyoudesire,andyousenditwhereyouwil
l.aimmyroadonyourbowofhopeandinafrenzyiwillfreemyfl
ockofarrows.onallsidesiseeyourwaistoffog,andyoursilence
huntsdownmyafflictedhours;mykissesanchor,andmymous

X

Always I fell
a book at your feet

You're sad
with me between your hands

Remember that sun fiesta
far away ago?

Who were we then
so lovewhole and burned?

I cruise in cool
dressed as a marine
heroically and all at once
like *sweet*

I charge with lunar energy
am hard for the climate
drunk on greywater

I make sounds
We're bent on madness!
Insanity!
Death!

Abandon your passion
for burning toxicating spray

Go solar

Watch as I pine infinitely
for the electric
throatfish upstream

I yield to no naked body

But fortunately for you you can
practice kissing on me

VIII

Ah I'm drunk and barefoot and I've come
to sleep on your belly
Honey
I've got a real buzz from the smoke
I had in the street
Ah I'm deep sick and naked
complaining in spirals of creaks
I long for your lap like home
Honey
I'm drunk-sick you're here-absent
I'm again again again

VII

Leaning on a lighthouse
I regard your afternoon eyes
shedding shadow

Night lengthens itself
just to fling about you

From the coast I send out
oceanic

drowning my sadman dread

VI

I remember the bonfire climbing
a house far off from the houses

My memory is always autumn

Yours hyacinth blue

We once fought and fell in a pond
clasping arms
revolving

Garnered a deep
thirsty thirst
for water

V

Will you?
My words

from grapes
my hands

stained
from grapes

I am
to blame

Follow me
like an old

hurricane
to the beach

IV

The storm is war
and I wave a white kerchief –

topple because of no
substance

no mass

Trees pulse with spray
without
weight

to language the wind

III

I use my voice to
break your ears
with
love frenzy
and *moist desire*

Can't you feel your lovesoul
dying?

Thus
I toll transparent
in the wheat for you

transparent in the wheat for you
in the wheat for you

with my
vast and moist and
RESONANT mouth

II

Old and mortal
mourn the ruined day

Great

It comes out again
this abstracted blue that wraps you

dark blue
pallid blue
flower blue
fire blue
sun blue
and I revolve around you

I

To survive the ache
I dig and persist in moss

Crushing weapon of your absence
you forged me
slow and sad

I was alone
and was alone
and am

a surrendered noun in a boundless noun

IN A BURNING BUILDING THE AIR
INSIDE IS HEATED BY FIRE AND
SO BECOMES LIGHTER

WATER MISTS AND SPRAYS SO EFFECTIVE

Fog buries the hill
and I don't know how to mourn a cat

I'm quiet but dig
I know how to do that

with a pick and shovel
I dig deep for the dark

You cry for your cat and
I've never cried for a cat

Instead I put my hand on your back

Think of soil's nitrification
How raccoons will probably

dig her up
The fog buries us too

TERRAFORM

You and I crossed the ocean blue
in 1492
on a pair of birch-bark water-skis
slowly being digested
by gold-seeking wood mites
hell bent on new land
The next time you're 60% sure of something
be 100% sure you're 60% water
Crawling out of an archaic sea
we brought some of it with us
in our loose eukaryotic sacks
and at what point in a transition
does one thing become the other?
It's at this point that I'm asking
Think for a moment of the soil
spilled across the deck from your potting
My only regret is that we terraformed earth
in concrete rather than bamboo shoots or lemon rinds
Think for a moment about the opposing
breath of a plant
How many $12.99 breaths
from the convenience store down the street
will we bring into this house?
My goal is to be a voyeur of roses
I wonder if the thing in me
that makes me kill bugs
rather than scoop them with a flash card

to be thrown from the door
is the thing that makes me mean about the future
I've been training the cat to be a dinosaur
terrorizing the insects
in the jungle of our living room
The wood mites evolved into ladybugs –
little red shocks on our green

WATER IS FOUND AS ICE

I'm trying everything I can
to stop giving off heat

To stop my hair from growing
Wish I could trace your sad-face with a crayon

I imagine myself in cottage grass
smelling dew for its dirt

How long was your hair?

I've stopped mine from growing
I'm growing

Gunning for eleven feet
to excuse myself from doorways

Tonight we dream the firemen
both came and did not come

A TEMPERATURE IS REACHED WHEN THE MOLECULES ARE VIBRATING SO MUCH THAT THEY BREAK FREE OF THEIR RIGID FRAMEWORK

Let's steep our bodies overnight
in the carriage of a caravan

I'll steal or borrow without returning – return it
to some river near the ocean

We'll retire our phones to cupholders and beyond the valley
the river can call out to the sound

Half asleep you'll tell me that of all the parking lots
you've slept in this one is by far your favourite

and when we wake to find a black bear in the plum tree
eating the plums we planned for breakfast

I'll point to the purple skins in its shit –
pretend to know more about bears than I do

Where are the pits?

Let's pretend I'll have answers
Let's pretend August doesn't chew its way into fall
Let's wait until the ringing stops

before admitting what it is that causes big animals
to strip fruit from all the trees

DAISY BUCHANAN

In bed naked
it's hot out
the window AC
makes me feel like Gatsby
makes me want
a dry martini
in a shallow *verre*
but I'll just chew
ice cubes
and burn a few calories
like this
The heat tries
to get in
bed naked
reading pirated PDFs
about how life's existence
can be explained
by thermodynamics
and equations that appear
written in sand
It all seems to be about
energy and communication –
even snowflakes can be
understood to be living
I like that
crush an ice cube
and touch my swampy parts

My last three texts
are you coming home tonight?
and well are you?
It's hot here on the lake

EXPAND, WHILE THE OUTER FACE REMAINS COOL

From what was left
we retrieved the typewriter
the wood trunk

The obvious metaphor

of your Blundstones
melted to the floor

Remember how the breathing-mask
straps left soft tracks

across your cheeks

how they faded by lunch
warm waking sleepmarks

IMAGINE TWO SOLID RODS, BOTH THE SAME LENGTH AND WIDTH, ONE MADE OF WOOD AND ONE IRON

In Northeast B.C.
a mayfly hatching
dense enough to stain
the weather report

Tent poles:
how your mother got
the year she didn't eat
How jeans and hair fell from her

Balanced on the tracks
look at the sky
past the cedar tips
Ignore the train's keen

Tell me again please
how light from the stars
hits us harder
than it feels

A GOING AWAY FROM A COMING TOWARD

I want to be in a South American painting
in a hot alley where not much happens
where we buy blood oranges
from a woman under a parasol
and eat on a stoop our feets in the street

In a plane I remember I don't understand
how Earth's invisible electromagnetic field works
or how birds can see it with their eyes
those forever migrants

If we flew around the world chasing sunset
every hour could be magic hour
No pasa nada

You tweak my thoughts to you the way gravity
from the unseen planet in our solar system
throws all the other orbits off a bit
dragging them toward it

To cure depression in 1887
docs would spin patients around on a stool until dizzy
in order to rearrange the contents of the brain

Can I borrow your face for a while to stare in a mirror?
By the time this universe ends there will be more years
than particles in existence
That might be time enough

I spent the day on the beach collecting every pink plastic
particle laying them out in the sand
as the pinwheel arms of our galaxy
I realize now I should have built a hard heart
Should have used shells

WHETHER IT IS SLOW, FAST, OR INHERENTLY VIOLENT

Wake to find
it is fall

Synapses fracture or fractal down
stairs

Put on the pants
with the belt

looped in them
Warm worn pockets

In my adult life
I've never held

a baby
I hear they smell soft

The thumbnail
is a tooth

is a splinter
is a touch-screen –

The books dress in
dust

our dust
So there's that

A clock-heart
beats above us

Check forty times for
a quarter-past-nine

Check forty times
to find it is fall

A BODY CANNOT BE MEASURED DIRECTLY

I want to count everything
that stems
from your
you:

toes
eyelashes

ideas
like antlers
made of space / time

Your small teeth

The talks that breathe
past them

THIS IS NOT CONFINED TO WATER ALONE

I try on your panties
so you are the boy

Got blue gifts and
rug burns
at eight

Poked dead things down by the creek

On a cold floor tight and fluorescent
it isn't sexual
yet

Feels like the view
from a falling
camera

Nakedness like dead things near water
a wet cold on skin near cold water

I try on your panties
as you watch
from the shower

and it isn't sexual yet

ALTHOUGH IN A SOLID THEY VIBRATE AROUND A FIXED POSITION

I

The man upstairs starts to vacuum
at first moan

Let's make sure his place
is spotless

2

Do we really need drapes?
A metal bed frame?

I've gone my whole life
without a juicer

But they enter my home
Are strange in our home

3

A streetlamp dies above us
The same dark we brought

in our pockets
The same dark in our

mouths and throats
we brought from home

4

You forget things
Leave the stove on twice a week

We don't talk about smoke
Just open windows

Let the inside air out

HEADS ARE SEALED GLASS BULBS FULL OF LIQUID

Needle through pleat
less poke and pierce
more a gliding –

A boy intent in tall grass

His face surfacing a dark lake
in three separate frames

Gum in the urinal
Sunlight at dusk

Some dusks I wonder
what it would be like

to bathe with Serge Gainsbourg
while he sings to young women

I'd like you to wash me and have it not sexy
but here the bathwater freezes

How wind hurts
Push a body through winter

THE ATTRACTIVE FORCE, OR FORCE OF COHESION, TENDS TO BIND THEM TOGETHER

The toilet bowl chips like a tooth so
we'll piss in the sink for a week

Hold the counter as if it's a branch

high enough to hurt if you fell
Swing your bony legs

I want to see grass-stained knees
Fill my mouth with leaves

THE SUN PASSES THROUGH EMPTY SPACE TO WARM THE EARTH

If I'm a horizon
you're a horizon
and there's a barn house between us
with two teens rolling around
in the hay
nearly almost just seeing
each other's fast flat black streaks
Cough / lozenge tooth knock /
a leaning toward the weeds
in the water
You yell at the lake
as it freezes over
Plastic-smoke / Fuck /
Six months
all my shit
still smells like a burning
You note that in moonlight
we're just a second surface
for the sun
to reflect itself off

POSSESSED BY A BODY DUE TO ITS POSITION

Why don't I yell my fetishes from the opposite shore
of a frozen lake to see if you hear them?
Send smoke signals back as ten-four?

I promise to wash my cumrags weekly

There was this conversation today:
Occam's razor as a case for Christianity
so lately I've been thinking of selling my organs

Send towels
a tub of ice

The light makes things look like L.A.

Someone told me the Segway
is the way of the future
so I started thinking of my dad dying

but ate some birthday cake instead
Darling

tell me
how many more times

will I open the oven with my glasses on?
At what point does martyrdom begin to pay off?

Darling
remember that time I could speak only
one sentence at a time?

It's happening again

THE MASS IS A BIG STEP TOWARD IDENTIFYING

A something ran down the roof last night

Maybe an unpinned pinecone
taking its time on the shingles

a lot like the rattle under the hood
we didn't discuss driving back

Outside in your white slip
flashlit

Me in underwear with a knife in my hand
You went out first so what does that say?

We saw nothing
so spent the night thinking of

the weight of water in the oceans
smoke slipping through cracks

IF TODAY AND TODAY I AM THINKING OF YOU

When I think of you entering the sea at dawn in the distance

It's easy to forget about seafoam kind of grossly adhering to
    your legs

Or strips of bull kelp lazy whipping the surf

And the fact that salt is two dangerous atoms stuck together

Imagination both is and is not outside the body

Fever is how the body reacts

Today I forgot to spend my life with you

Breaking into the city's swimming pools

With friends with tight bodies who know

How to spend their lives not just thinking

Halfway through my five-year plan I remember all the bees

Are dying from fever so cut it to figure out what we'll do

Tomorrow: a blanket / a car / open space –

Should I file this love poem between the first and fortieth?

We could take our bodies to the ocean to sink it

Because like air this is quiet and happens in the corners

THIS UNBALANCED CONDITION IS RESPONSIBLE FOR A FORCE WHICH DRIVES

I've been drinking NyQuil to fall asleep
remembering the 141 near Huntsville at night
as sleep pulls up from behind

The most precious thing
I saw this year
was a little paisley girl plug her ears
when a wasp flew near her
A winter wasp flew near her
a wasp near her ears in winter

The thing about the 141 near Huntsville
is how many cigarettes I've smoked
on the side of the 141
waiting for an older man to pick me up
in his F-150 late in winter

My hands in my pockets
though my ears are cold
I want to cover my ears on the 141
but my hands in my pockets

Or my hands and cigarettes
My hands in a truck behind a boatyard
and how behind a boatyard
we smoked and drank cough syrup

I want you to know how in winter
behind a boatyard under some trees
I smoked and drank NyQuil
to fall asleep

SOME MOLECULES WILL RE-ENTER THE LIQUID

It's Thursday
the soup's on

I hope it feeds us
'til Sunday

so we aren't always
at the sandwich place

eating $6.50 sandwiches
in the window

I put vegetables in
green and orange

and chicken
It boils

particles hot
and crashing

so the window
waters up

I look out
at other buildings

their power lines
and windows

Before we were born

your mother stood
in a closet

before the sun rose
smelling flannels

Think of the yard
we can have

once we move us

The garden we'll have
eating light

The garden with
green-orange vegetables

I'll watch you
run your hand through

from a window

How we'll tack
all our clothes

to the walls

ANXIOUS AVOIDANT

When you are sad
and you are sad
your eyelids pink
to the shade of your lips
eyelips
speaking in breaths
between the blinking

I am summer scum
this summer
missing your stoned texts –

*I carried a single shoe
around Value Village for an hour*

*trying to find its partner
slain in an aisle somewhere*

The most intimate thing I did this summer
was match someone
both on Bumble and Tinder
and never say anything
at all

The texts I get now –

Here

Here

Downstairs

Slain in an aisle somewhere

POUR A GLASS HALF FULL INTO A BIGGER GLASS

Mouth cracked
and bleeding a little
at the side
what happens now
when I practice making out
with my hand
the way I did in grade school
far too passionate
'til someone saw me red

I'm that cruise ship
the drunk captain shored
on rocks off the coast of Italy
a few years ago
tide sucking in and out
the open windows
Or maybe a frozen tide

I don't delete the last grocery list
from my phone
find it
when a night is alone
Lysol
3 lmns
wax paper
bags of ice

I never wanted to borrow
your sweater
just wanted to be in it with you
tight arms and all
but there's this
head-caught-in-the-sleeve panic
to it all
this one-two-three quality
to it all
we never quite sort out

Cigarette wink lit
can't stop forcing myself
to feel tragic
so I chew a sunset Percocet
on the deck
You always found that
funnysad
like valentine candy hearts
me 2
i luv u
plz b my type
of salvation

ARMISTICE

Give me hackneyed words because they are good
— Lisa Robertson

Give me hackneyed words because they are
what's left in the end
Give you landscape – silo – sky
A dead lawn covered in Old Milwaukee cans
a kiddie pool and *Playboys* from the eighties
Give me dirty texts from a pay phone
using Morse code and quarters
Sometimes it's good to be on sidewalks
not just walking
but don't actually
give me anything please
I haven't been on Harbord Street for months
If sunset in winter was a place
I'd move there today

Give me a pay phone a sun in winter
give me a thread
If I can't write a poem
about the CEO of Segway™
being thrown from a cliff by a Segway™
throw me from a cliff
plz & thx
If I can't write a poem
about a man's love at first selfie
on the toilet while on Tinder™
with who is to become his first wife
throw me from a cliff
plz & thx
xoxo

Today the sun broke through the clouds
and as it hit my hackneyed skin
in the parking lot of a Best Buy
while I looked at my new
forty-two-inch HDTV
that not only records shows and movies
but plays out their every possible plot line
in every infinite way
I was filled with almost-joy
Disney's newest trope is that all the princes
drink and self-destruct
and need a girl wearing denim to save them –
Denim Deb and the Self-Loathing Prince Stuck Up a Tree
In my favourite of the shows Ernest Hemingway
drinks and self-destructs
and suicides himself in the head

Give me a hackneyed word for the feeling
of not being able to start eating
until something on my forty-two-inch HDTV is playing
Hate the future but love my two-dollar burgers
and high-speed streaming funnies
Who knew creating a new Netflix password
was going to be the most trying
part of everything
I watched six seasons of *Weeds* in six days
fell in love with Mary-Louise Parker
and bad acting

Give me BuzzFeed Advice on
How to Get Over Your Ex in Ten Days like
1) Take Risks!
so I spat off a bridge
I flicked a coin into a well
bit the Hot Pocket straight from the oven
so I called your mother finally
I pushed all the elevator buttons in a skyrise
imagined a conversation where I said no to my boss
littered in the subway
so I didn't wear a helmet
so I stopped crossing streets in designated crossing areas
so I fed a raccoon some Pringles
checked Craigslist for desirables
2) Be Adventurous!
so I watched porn I don't want to discuss

Give me the time you said you wished
more things were crepuscular
so you could hear the word more often
I can crawl around on all fours for you
when the sun sets and rises
You can call me what you want
I learned that at the top of a highrise
the sun sets later and rises earlier
than for those of us on the ground
If you've ever heard a better excuse
for booking the Presidential
or having your head located
above your shoulders
let me hear it

Newton sorted a lot of stuff out
because he asked the prettiest questions
Does the Moon Also Fall?
I know he was talking
about an apple
but if he wasn't
such a virgin
it might have been him falling
Why is it I can never say things pretty?
The flower shorn
A murmur divided

Give me help with how to think about science
From below the ice of a frozen lake
wouldn't a bird's shadow seem like flight anyway?
There really aren't
that many mediums
just a lot of space
and space within those mediums
an atom is 99% empty
I hope you don't believe me
when I tell you I spent
the last year
watching videos on YouTube
about space and mediums
because what a dumb thing to say
to anyone after a year
of not saying anything
After a year of nothing
in a something

Give you the summer
summer air and the geese
were caught in the algae
So it's back to the fan
like last year and last year's
last year:
how closer to the centre
the faster the spinning
The hair in your face
Our limbs like on fire
Lily leaves near the shelf
The idea of swallowing
a copper wire
to run through the red tunnels
of my body
so when you'd position me
palms up I'd stay put

Death is just about entropy
Death is about just entropy
Death is entropy about just
is about just Death entropy
entropy Death is about just
just Death entropy about is
entropy about Death just is
entropy just is Death about
just Death is entropy about
is Death entropy just about
is just about Death entropy
just Death about is entropy
just is about entropy Death
entropy is just Death about
about Death just is entropy
entropy Death is just about
is Death just about entropy
is about Death entropy just
just about entropy is Death
Death about just entropy is
is Death about just entropy
just entropy is Death about
about is just entropy Death
about just entropy Death is
just about is entropy Death
about entropy is just Death
about Death entropy just is
entropy is Death just about
just entropy Death about is
just about entropy Death is

Give me the time you called me
fuckboy – softboy – softbones
Your kinky mess
There are things wrong with me
my greatest weakness
that I care
too much
that I work
too much
am just
too much of a damn team player
But an intense commitment to cognitive dissonance
is my most valuable asset

I signed up for this webinar
that teaches you
how to feel things right
it's called
no one has any idea what they're fucking doing:
an exploration in faking it / making it
I heard a bee vibrate
in a desperate attempt to communicate
to the bee next to it
and thought it was my phone
thought it was you
I hate bees and you more now
I'm such a millennial whore

Give me hangovers I've learned to love
like crap friends from high school
who need things like a ride or an invite
or for you to apologize for their behaviour –
They're not normally this bad
We don't really hang out much
I promise I won't see them again
I promise
I promise
I need need a drink with a cute umbrella in it

Give me give me
and pretty petty partly pretty
a flower shorn of half its petals
is still a flower just shorn of half its petals
The vet back from Iraq with one leg not quite there
dreams of swimming circles 'round the watering hole
The blue / yellow pills in this countryside –
little wish-coins down the well
of my wholesome throat

I know you can see
cities from space
can you see the shawarma place
I'm in,
West Toronto?
Eating wraps now that
the pizza tastes like you
but $2 slices come on
The mitosis of a swallow's murmuration
along the lake's frozen horizon
the wholeness
of things divided
things divisible
like a murmur
Pain – please stop gyrating your waist in my face
Memory – I'll call you tomorrow

Whether we weather the electron storm
is no longer of any importance –
but batten down the hatches
still I guess
Jupiter's rust-coloured storm
has been cranking for four hundred years
but it's shrinking
This is the emergency present
Just another day I think I recognize
everyone everywhere
and miss everything that's ever happened
all at once

NOTES AND ACKNOWLEDGEMENTS

'~~Veinte~~': All of the text in this section was taken from a 1969 copy of Pablo Neruda's *Twenty Love Poems and a Song of Despair*, translated by W. S. Merwin. Each poem is composed with only words found in the original poem. The visual poem is the entire book typed out with no spaces, each page laid on top of the previous pages.

'In a Burning Building the Air inside Is Heated by Fire and so Becomes Lighter': Most of the titles included in this section are fragments of sentences taken directly from *The Fire Service Manual Volume 1, Physics and Chemistry for Firefighters*.

'This is the emergency present' is a line taken directly from a Facebook post made by Marc Di Saverio.

Earlier versions of some of these poems have appeared in *Plenitude Magazine*, *The Mackinac*, *Prism International*, and *Metatron Omega*, and in the chapbooks ~~Veinte~~ (Vallum Chapbooks Series) and *In a Burning Building the Air inside Is Heated by Fire and so Becomes Lighter* (Desert Pets Press).

For their support throughout everything and all of this I'd like to thank my parents, Chris Gudgeon, Catriona Wright, Michael Nardone, Peter Gizzi, Vincent Colistro, and Hilary McLean. For taking such care in truly shaping and forming this book, I'd like to thank Karen Solie. Thank you to Writer's Trust of Canada for the financial support. Thank you for reading.

Vincent Pagé has had work published in *Prism*, *Geist*, *The Malahat Review*, *Metatron*, *Event*, *The Puritan*, and *Vallum*, among other journals. He was nominated for a National Magazine Award in 2015.

Typeset in Aragon and Gotham

Printed at the Coach House on bpNichol Lane in Toronto, Ontario, on Zephyr Antique Laid paper, which was manufactured, acid-free, in Saint-Jérôme, Quebec, from second-growth forests. This book was printed with vegetable-based ink on a 1973 Heidelberg KORD offset litho press. Its pages were folded on a Baumfolder, gathered by hand, bound on a Sulby Auto-Minabinda, and trimmed on a Polar single-knife cutter.

Edited for the press by Karen Solie
Designed by Alana Wilcox and Crystal Sikma
Cover by Crystal Sikma
Cover art by Lee Joseph McClure
Author photo by Limn Design

Coach House Books
80 bpNichol Lane
Toronto ON M5S 3J4
Canada

416 979 2217
800 367 6360

mail@chbooks.com
www.chbooks.com